W9-ACE-833

The Fourth Estate

Journalism in North America

Television News and the 24-Hour News Cycle

Kristin Thiel

Cavendish
Square

New York

Published in 2019 by Cavendish Square Publishing, LLC
243 5th Avenue, Suite 136, New York, NY 10016

Copyright © 2019 by Cavendish Square Publishing, LLC

First Edition

Library of Congress Cataloging-in-Publication Data

Names: Thiel, Kristin, 1977- author.
Title: Television news and the 24-hour news cycle / Kristin Thiel.
Description: New York : Cavendish Square, 2019. | Series: The fourth estate: journalism in North America | Includes bibliographical references and index. | Audience: Grade 7 to 12.
Identifiers: LCCN 2018000511 (print) | LCCN 2018004334 (ebook) | ISBN 9781502634924 (eBook) | ISBN 9781502634917 (library bound) | ISBN 9781502634931 (pbk.) | ISBN 9781502634948 (6-pack)
Subjects: LCSH: Television broadcasting of news--United States--Juvenile literature.
Classification: LCC PN4784.T4 (ebook) | LCC PN4784.T4 T475 2019 (print) | DDC 070.1/95--dc23
LC record available at https://lccn.loc.gov/2018000511

Editorial Director: David McNamara
Editor: Caitlyn Miller
Copy Editor: Nathan Heidelberger
Associate Art Director: Amy Greenan
Designer: Joe Parenteau
Production Coordinator: Karol Szymczuk
Photo Research: J8 Media

CONTENTS

The Fourth Estate

Journalism in North America

Before twenty-four-hour television programming, stations showed test patterns like this at night.

Television News: Twenty-Four Hours a Day

For television's first couple of decades, viewers were lucky if they picked up signals for ABC, CBS, NBC, and PBS. Those channels ran programming only a few hours each day. At some point each night, the stations went to static or an off-the-air pattern. There is a saying that the news never sleeps. However, television networks did.

Then, on June 1, 1980, everything changed. The Cable News Network (CNN) became the first twenty-four-hour news station. Before CNN, if an event happened outside of limited broadcast hours, the public would not hear about it until hours later. The new twenty-four-hour news cycle meant that reporters were always investigating, and the network was always broadcasting the latest news.

This change did not appear out of thin air. A lot of smaller changes—in public perception of news, television technology, television rules, and economic factors—happened first. What did not change was human hunger for information. People have long wanted what the twenty-four-hour news cycle promises to deliver. They have always wanted the news as fast as possible.

The Telegraph: Preparing for Twenty-Four-Hour News

The twenty-four-hour news cycle is considered a modern innovation that started because of the power of television. Before the internet, television was the first technology to allow news to reach people as it happened. However, in many ways, the twenty-four-hour news cycle is hardly a new idea.

The "obsession" with the news started with the telegraph in the mid-1800s. Historian David Hochfelder has written extensively about the changes the telegraph brought. He says, "We can locate the roots of today's obsession with the news cycle in the telegraphic dispatches."

The telegraph was one of the first technologies to facilitate communication over long distances. Samuel Morse sent the first message by telegraph in 1844. In that dispatch, Morse wrote a line from the Bible: "What hath God wrought!" In other words, Morse wondered what he had done. He knew there would be big consequences

With the advent of the telegraph in 1844, news could travel faster than ever before.

because of his invention. In his second message, Morse wrote, "Have you any news?" Morse knew he would no longer have to wait days, weeks, or months for news to reach him by messengers or in newspapers.

The implications were staggering. When the American Civil War started in 1861, soldiers sent telegrams to newspaper offices in major cities. Crowds would gather to read these messages. Writer Oliver Wendell Holmes called this "war fever." He said people could not do anything but think of the news. One of Holmes's friends told him that he suffered from this "fever." His friend "would read the same telegraphic dispatches over and over again in different papers, as if they were new, until he felt as if he were an idiot."

That sounds a lot like how people respond to information in the twenty-first century. We constantly refresh social media, watch recaps of stories we have already read about—and leave the television on twenty-four hours a day.

The Invention of Television

The telegraph is considered part of the same chain of communications technology that television belongs to. From telegraph to telephone to television, each innovation built on the last. Early inventors sending audio over long distances dreamed of next sending visuals long distances—like today's video phone calls. In 1884, German scientist Paul G. Nipkow received a patent for his electric telescope. It turned the light of a moving image into an electrical signal that could be sent from place to place across a wire. Three years later, in 1887, German physicist Heinrich Rudolf Hertz figured out what naturally occurring radio waves were. Those electromagnetic waves were what allowed television to broadcast. As early as the 1880s, magazine articles and cartoons depicted the futuristic possibilities of what we would now consider television.

Though television technology has been around since the 1920s, widespread commercial development of television sets did not happen until after 1945. Those early televisions were 4 to 10 inches (10 to 25 centimeters) across. They showed grainy, black-and-white images from three broadcast networks. They were so expensive that they were out of reach for many families.

By the time the United States was involved in World War II, ten thousand sets had been sold to the American public. The war slowed down television production because the military needed those factories to produce parts for the war effort, but it would soon pick up again. By 1950, there were about six million sets in American homes; by 1960, there were almost sixty million. In 2004, television sets were big, sometimes hanging on walls like movie screens. They showed high-definition images sent by hundreds of broadcast, cable, and satellite networks. Yet they were also affordable enough for 98 percent of American households to have at least one television set. This technology has come a long way in a short amount of time.

The Language of Television

The first mention of the word "television" was at the 1900 World's Fair. It is from the Greek "tele," which means "distant," and the Latin "visio," which means "sight." So "television" means "seeing at a distance." For a long time, one of the big debates about the technology was around the name. Many people hated the word "television." They suggested "radioscope," "farscope," "mirascope," "optiphone," and "lustreer." No one could agree on what to call the television audience either. "Viewer" today seems so straightforward, but through the 1930s, people debated the terms "lookers-in," "perceptors," "audiobservers," "telegazers," and "audivists."

Three of those terms made it to the US Patent and Trademark Office. Two men, working separately, officially developed what we would call the modern television set, though they used different words for it. Vladimir Zworykin was an immigrant from Russia who worked at Westinghouse, an American electrical equipment manufacturer. In 1923, he received a patent for what he called an "iconoscope," an electric eye. This was a camera tube, the heart of the television. The screen he developed was called the "kinescope." Put together, they transmitted images electronically in 1925, the first time that had ever happened. Despite this success, Westinghouse told him to stop working on television technology. The company did not think it would be a valuable invention. Westinghouse was wrong, of course. Seven decades later, in 1995, Westinghouse would buy CBS; in 1999, the media conglomerate Viacom would buy Westinghouse.

There was another person who developed modern television technology at the same time. Philo T. Farnsworth started experimenting with television technology when he was only fourteen years old, in 1921. By the time he was twenty, in 1927, he had a patent for what he called the "image dissector." He knew who might be most interested in his invention and first presented his idea to the San Francisco media. Though Farnsworth's invention did not become the industry standard, today he is remembered by many as the "father of electronic television."

Bringing Television to the Masses

The public first saw television technology in action on April 7, 1927. Bell Laboratories and the US Department of Commerce broadcast the image and voice of Herbert Hoover, who was then the US secretary of commerce and would go on to become president of the United States in 1929. According to *The Broadcast Century and Beyond: A Biography of American Broadcasting,* the *New York Times* reported on the event. The newspaper wrote, "Herbert Hoover made a speech in Washington yesterday afternoon. An audience in New York heard him and saw him. More than 200 miles [320 kilometers] of space intervening between the speaker and his audience was annihilated by the television apparatus ... It was as if a photograph had suddenly come to life."

However, the public was not ready for television to be their primary home entertainment source, and television technology was not ready either. Radio was still incredibly popular. Companies were still learning about the science behind televisions. The government was making rules about communications technology, like establishing the Federal Communications Commission (FCC). They also had to sort out the dueling patents of Zworykin and Farnsworth.

Finally, television sets were still too expensive for most people to afford. This was enough of a concern that one media company tried to do something about it. The Radio Corporation of America (RCA) was one of the largest manufacturers of radios, but by the mid-1920s, it was getting into television. It launched NBC radio in 1926, which would turn into NBC television. RCA launched a million-dollar three-part program in 1935 with the goal of manufacturing affordable television sets. This plan, spearheaded by RCA's president, David Sarnoff, tried to solve issues of production and promotion. The company moved its production of television sets to factory assembly lines. Making more sets faster and more efficiently would lower their cost to consumers. RCA knew no one would buy a set, even if it was affordable, if there were no interesting television shows to watch. So the company also added programs to its NBC television network. Finally, RCA knew no one could buy or watch if they did not know what television was. The company planned to demonstrate television to large crowds. RCA went big in that department. It revealed its work at the 1939 World's Fair in New York. Its first broadcast from there was of President Franklin D. Roosevelt's speech that opened the fair. This made Roosevelt the first sitting president to appear on television.

All of RCA's work resulted in eight different companies, including RCA, stepping forward to sell television sets to the public in 1939. The cost was still high, and the Great Depression, which had financially devastated many families, had only recently ended. Still, five thousand sets were sold that year alone. The public believed in the technology, even if they had to save money from elsewhere in their budgets. Over the next decades, television's popularity would explode, and that popularity would pave the way for television news.

The Changing Perception of News

In 1962, Walter Cronkite was chosen to anchor the CBS *Evening News*. The program was only fifteen minutes long at the time. The next year, CBS would be the first network to expand its nightly news to thirty minutes. According to a 2012 article from CNN, Cronkite made his bosses angry with his very first broadcast. He ended his fifteen-minute report with this advice to viewers: "That's the news. Be sure to check your local newspapers tomorrow to get all of the details on the headlines we're delivering to you." Even the anchor of a television news program believed newspapers still provided the best in-depth coverage of world and national events.

However, several groundbreaking events would soon start to change that opinion. Cronkite's biographer, Douglas Brinkley, says 1968 became "one of the most talked about years in US history." The United States was involved in the Vietnam War. Martin Luther King Jr. and Robert Kennedy were assassinated. There were violent protests at the Democratic National Convention in Chicago. Richard Nixon won an intense presidential election. Space exploration went far—literally, as the first spacecraft with astronauts aboard left Earth's orbit and sent back photos taken from space. Cronkite covered all those stories and played "a central role in that year," Brinkley says.

Cronkite began to use his power to "set the agenda" for news coverage. He flew to Vietnam. He did his own reporting on the war. He formed his own opinions on it and told the American people what he thought, which "had a transformative effect on the country," according to Brinkley. He was also a key figure in the creation of the Environmental Protection Agency. On January 1, 1970, Cronkite announced that the news had to start talking about the environment. He started a segment called "Can We Save the Planet?" It aired every night.

Because the public felt they could trust Cronkite, they began to trust television news. Because he wanted to

Richard Hubbell: The First Television News Anchor

"No one remembers Richard Hubbell," says a Poynter Institute article. The journalism school's history of the early days of television news demonstrates how quickly the media landscape shifts—and how many figures from those early days have been forgotten.

Hubbell, the first news anchor, is largely unknown for many reasons. There is even some disagreement if Hubbell was, in fact, the first anchor. Some say a man named Lowell Thomas anchored the first television news broadcast. Thomas's program was called *Sunoco News*, broadcast on what is now NBC. However, Thomas's show was simply a simulcast of his radio program. Hubbell was the first person to host a news program that aired exclusively on television.

Richard Hubbell and the News began in 1941, when only a few thousand homes in the United States had televisions. It ran twice a week on New York City's WCBW, a station that is now CBS. Each episode was fifteen minutes long. Hubbell's program ended when the United States entered World War II. Then, radio was a much more developed technology than television was. The important news of the war was best shared by radio, and it would be ten to twenty years until television became a

Opposite: Richard Hubbell reports for CBS on November 5, 1941.

major player in the news. For example, television networks first covered the national conventions for the presidential race in 1952. In 1960, a debate between presidential candidates John F. Kennedy and Richard M. Nixon was broadcast on radio and, for the time first, on television. People who only listened to the debate thought Nixon had done better than Kennedy; those who could also see the candidates, by watching on television, thought Kennedy had won the debate. This difference showed television's power to affect perception and opinion.

steer the news in a certain direction, the news began to have a personality. All of this set the foundation for the future of television news.

Early Anchor Wars

In 1980, the twenty-four-hour news cycle was just beginning. However, it was not the only exciting thing happening in television news at that time. Dan Rather replaced Walter Cronkite as anchor of the CBS *Evening News* the next year. This was the first major, and controversial, change in network news.

Cronkite had became known as the "most trusted man in America." He was already famous for his coverage of many defining moments in American history. Cronkite's calm delivery of major stories was remarkable and is considered especially important because the emotional events of the Cronkite era affected everyone in the United States and most of the world.

Yet as the 1970s drew to a close, CBS was poised to make a big change. At the time, Rather was a top CBS journalist. The network feared he was going to quit his job with CBS and start reporting for ABC. In 1980, CBS made a move to keep Rather on staff. The network offered him $2.2 million as well as the job of CBS *Evening News* anchor.

The switch from Cronkite to Rather created shock waves that reached both the media and the public. The controversy continued until Rather was replaced in 2005. Then, Cronkite told CNN that he never thought Rather should have had the anchor job. He wished someone like journalist Bob Schieffer had taken over his job. He thought Rather had just been "playing a role," not truly being the anchor.

Dan Rather, then a CBS correspondent, reports on the Kennedy assassination on November 23, 1963.

This kind of competition became the rule, not the exception, in television news. In the 1980s, the anchors of the evening news on the three major network channels famously drew their own fiercely loyal audiences. As a 1986 *Rolling Stone* magazine article titled "Anchor Wars" explained, in many ways ABC's, CBS's, and NBC's news programming appeared the same. Their evening news anchors—Peter Jennings, Dan Rather, and Tom Brokaw, respectively—were all white males of similar ages and with similar off-camera lives. They all helmed programs of the same length with the same format and shown at the same time. They even each received the same size audience. Yet many viewers remained committed to one anchor over another. *Rolling Stone* said, "Viewers have read the implicit iconography of the evening news and aligned themselves in accordance with their understanding of the subtext of each man and program." In the 1980s, a family was a Jennings family, a Rather family, or a Brokaw family, without deviation. Similarly, in the twenty-first century, viewers have drawn lines among the morning news programs like *Good Morning America*, *CBS This Morning*, and the *Today* show. Audience preference as well as behind-the-scenes contract negotiations, anchor personality clashes, and legal issues pit news anchors against each other regularly.

Changing Technology

President John F. Kennedy's death in 1963 was the major event that encouraged media organizations to invest in technology. Radio programs could not show what was happening. Newspapers could not go to print fast enough to keep up with rapidly developing stories. Only television news could provide a complete picture—with audio *and* visuals—immediately.

However, the available technology in the early 1960s did not make television news crews' jobs easy. Filming live events took a lot of planning. It was not as simple as holding up a cell phone and hitting "record." Television studios needed to get large trucks filled with bulky equipment to the scene. Also, there were no satellites to beam video around the world. Television producers worked hard to get film from the scene of Kennedy's assassination in Dallas, Texas, to the network studios, which would then transmit the images to the nation and the world. As a result, in the 1970s, videotape began replacing film. Video translated easier to air than film did. Mobile newsrooms allowed local stations to go live at the scene of an event much quicker than ever before.

The network C-SPAN started televising US political proceedings in 1979. By 1982, its cameras were broadcasting events like US House sessions twenty-four hours a day. Television's commitment to new technology like the videotape made this twenty-four-hour coverage possible.

Changing Rules

Cable television technology has been around since the 1940s. In fact, for some households in those early days of television, cable was the only option available. Broadcast television was so young that it was not everywhere. According to *The Presidency in the Era of 24-Hour News*, fourteen thousand homes had cable in 1952. Cable spread fast in those first years. At the time, the Federal Communications Commission (FCC) regulated broadcasting but not cable. This meant that cable could grow surprisingly quickly. However, there was one factor that slowed cable's growth: the infrastructure for cable cost a lot more to build than broadcasting did. Nonetheless, by 1963, cable had one million subscribers.

This scared broadcasters. They pressured the FCC to regulate cable too. For the rest of the 1960s, the FCC did a lot to control cable. These new rules kept cable television out of many households.

The landscape changed yet again in the 1970s. A decision by a federal appeals court in 1976 said the FCC could no longer regulate cable so heavily. By the mid-1980s, more than forty million homes in the United States subscribed to cable. In 1984, US Congress passed the Cable Act. The landmark legislation deregulated the cost of cable. In 1985, a federal appeals court removed FCC rules that required cable operators to carry all local broadcast signals.

The Economics of Television News

Television news is big business, and that means big money is involved. The advertising-news connection is a circle that feeds on itself. As soon as CNN started, it pulled a lot of the world's audience from broadcast channels. Advertisers followed. They liked not only the amount of people who watched CNN but also that the audience was a global one. Suddenly, they could easily sell their products all around the world. Before the internet, this was the first time companies could reach a global market.

Losing audiences and advertisers meant that broadcast television networks had to raise their ad fees. That, plus the perceived faster pace of twenty-four-hour cable channels, led to advertisers shortening their commercials from the standard thirty seconds to fifteen seconds.

Under Ronald Reagan's presidency, there was great tolerance of corporate media growth. News companies merged with companies making and selling products. In

1986, General Electric (GE) bought RCA, which owned NBC. Media was now connected with an appliance manufacturer. In 1989, Time and Warner Communications merged into Time Warner, which became a sprawling media conglomerate composed of everything from magazine companies to book publishers to cable television networks.

To this day, higher ratings equate to higher ad prices. When the public isn't watching the news, ad rates plummet and journalists lose their jobs. This means that newsrooms must care about attracting, and keeping, viewers. These economic factors still shape the form and content of the news we watch.

CNN: "Indispensable Wallpaper"

CNN stepped into the space that opened because of technology and rules that supported cable television technology. David Folkenflik, NPR's media correspondent, says that in the late 1970s and early 1980s, there was an untapped chance for the creation of another television network. ABC, CBS, and NBC had a good 80 percent of the whole country's television audience. However, each major city in the United States had at least three newspapers. There was an imbalance. There was, therefore, room for more television networks.

CNN's founder, Ted Turner, knew how to explain the necessity of his new network. He "sort of described [CNN] as a newspaper of the air," Folkenflik said. By couching CNN in terms the average American related to, Turner was able to show the world what was to be gained from television news.

The Twenty-Four-Hour News Cycle Explained Through Cartoons

Editorial cartoonists help people understand world events through drawings. They can also help people understand the news itself. John Deering and Nick Anderson have both drawn cartoons about twenty-four-hour news.

John Deering got his first cartooning job in 1981. The twenty-four-hour news cycle was starting around then too. In 2009, Deering published a cartoon about round-the-clock news. The cartoon shows ancient Egyptians experiencing a plague. Millions of frogs rain down on them. (The Bible includes a story that God sent this disaster to punish the Egyptians.) In the cartoon, the Egyptians are glad "the 24-hour cable news networks aren't around yet to flog this story." With this cartoon, Deering showed how pervasive twenty-four-hour news had become. He also offered the opinion that news coverage that never takes a break may not always be a good thing. A news story that has been "flogged" is one that has been talked about so much it is no longer interesting. Even a story as tremendous as God punishing a country with frog storms could be made boring by the relentless coverage of television news.

In 2014, Deering published a cartoon that shows Uncle Sam and a bald eagle watching television. The screen says, "You are watching your American justice system." The show is being brought to viewers by "TBM," which stands for "Trial by Media 24 Hour Network." Deering suggested that twenty-four-hour news coverage affects the news. The twenty-four-hour news cycle shares details fast and without any breaks. This can cause misinformation to spread.

Known for his editorial cartoons, John Deering has many artistic talents, including designing sculptures.

Nick Anderson has won a Pulitzer Prize for his editorial cartoons. In one of his 2009 cartoons, a four-legged wild tiger is labeled "24-hr news cycle." Two golf shoes and a golf club lie on the ground near the tiger's head. The tiger burps, indicating that he has just eaten. The cartoon is about golfer Tiger Woods, whose personal scandals—and their subsequent news coverage—damaged his reputation forever.

Turner seemed to reference newspapers in another way too. Because newspapers need some lead time to get a story out, they write obituaries for famous people before they die. This way, they are prepared to publish quickly when those people do die. In similar fashion, when Turner launched CNN, he also talked about how his network would end.

In an interview, he said, "We won't be signing off until the world ends. We'll be on, we'll be covering it live, and that will be our last, last event." Before the world ended, whenever that happened, CNN would play the song "Nearer My God to Thee." In 2015, the website *Jalopnik* obtained a video from the CNN archives titled "TURNER DOOMSDAY VIDEO—HFR till the end of the world confirmed." "HRF" stands for "hold for release." The video is about a minute long. In it, US military band members play "Nearer My God to Thee" outside the mansion Turner lived in in the 1980s. Turner had prepared the video so that his network was prepared for the ending of the world and its own final broadcast.

CNN founder Ted Turner viewed his new network's mission as pure and good. He has said that his one goal was always for the network to be the "best news network on the planet." It took a while for the rest of the media to give CNN the chance to blossom. When CNN started, the three major broadcast networks (ABC, CBS, and NBC) called it the Chicken Noodle Network. This nickname was meant negatively. Chicken noodle soup is often considered a basic, uncomplicated dish. CNN was similarly considered by many to have embarrassingly few resources, which competitors assumed meant CNN could not produce quality news programs. Slowly, CNN worked to be taken seriously. In 1987, CNN's first chief news anchor, Bernard Shaw, was included with Peter Jennings (anchor at ABC), Dan Rather (anchor at CBS), and Tom Brokaw (anchor at NBC) in a group interview with President Ronald Reagan. A few years after that, the networks were admitting that CNN was an important part of the news world. Folkenflik says that during the first Gulf War, in 1991, other networks started following CNN's lead. CNN "became sort of this indispensable wallpaper," Folkenflik says.

The people at CNN are just one piece of the rise of the twenty-four-hour news cycle. The reporters and anchors of early television news each played an important role in the medium's evolution. There are as many tellers as there are stories, but next we will learn more about a few of the early adopters of twenty-four-hour news.

CNN founder Ted Turner
speaks at an event in 1981.

The Storytellers

There are many storytellers in television news. It takes a lot of people to keep the twenty-four-hour news cycle going. Six people are among the most important "founders" of twenty-four-hour news. Five are related to CNN, the network that led the nonstop news revolution. Ted Turner started the network. Tom Johnson was CNN's president when it became famous. Bernard Shaw, Peter Arnett, and John Holliman were the journalists who scooped the story that solidified CNN's role in twenty-four-hour news. Other networks emerged in direct response to the success of CNN. One of the most prominent figures in American media today is Rupert Murdoch, the founder of Fox News.

Ted Turner: "Mouth of the South"

Robert Edward Turner III has had many nicknames. He has been called the Mouth of the South, Terrible Ted, and Captain Outrageous. Turner has called himself a maverick. He even titled his 1999 book *Ted Turner Speaks: Insights from the World's Greatest Maverick*. Tom Johnson, president of CNN in the early 1990s, called Turner the only genius he has ever known.

Turner was born in 1938 in Cincinnati, Ohio. From an early age, he went by Ted, a nickname for his middle name of Edward. Since he had the same name as his father, Robert Edward II, who was called Ed, this helped distinguish the two men.

After high school, Turner attended Brown University. He then served in the US Coast Guard. Turner has been married three times. He married for the first time in 1960. He and wife Judy Nye had two children before they divorced. In 1965, Turner married again. He and Janie Smith had three children together. In 1991, Turner got married for a third time, to Jane Fonda, a famous actor. They, too, eventually divorced.

Work

In 1963, Turner took over his dad's business. Turner Advertising Co. sold space on billboards for ads. Turner has said his secret to success is "Early to bed, early to rise, work like hell and advertise." However, advertising was not all he was interested in. By 1970, Turner knew he wanted his company to be about many different types of communication. He renamed it Turner Communications Group.

This new name allowed him to work in more types of media. He purchased two television stations: one in Atlanta, Georgia; the other in Charlotte, North Carolina. He named them WTCG and WRET. After the "W," which is a common part of a station's call sign, each letter stood for a word that was meaningful to Turner. WTCG was for "Turner Communications Group." WRET was for "Robert Edward Turner."

He then created a new station, Turner Broadcasting Systems. It became the United States' first "superstation." The channel TBS, as it is now known, used satellite technology to carry its signal across the country.

On June 1, 1980, Turner launched CNN. He already had a growing media empire. He knew he could use his power and money from that to accomplish more. His company continued to launch channels, including TNT in 1988, the Cartoon Network in 1992, Turner Classic Movies in 1994, and CNN en Español in 1997.

In 1996, Turner sold his company. Time Warner bought it. Turner kept leadership power, however, as vice-chairman of the company. He remained in that role until early 2003. He served on the company's board of directors until 2006.

Philanthropy

Turner believes it is important to donate a lot of his earnings to charity. In 2010, he joined thirty-nine other billionaires in a promise to leave at least half of their fortune to charity.

Turner's formal commitment to giving started twenty years before that. He started the Turner Foundation in 1990 in order to donate money to environmental causes. In 1997, he pledged $1 billion to the United Nations, to be paid over ten years. It took him eighteen years, but he fulfilled his promise in 2015. In 2001, Turner gave the US government $31 million to pay off its own debt to the United Nations. In 2007, he started investing in solar energy.

Sensationalism

Sensationalist news stories are more exciting or shocking than they are accurate. Newspeople share them with audiences to provoke them and to get them talking. In turn, news organizations hope to increase their subscriptions, ratings, and revenue. Sensationalism is nothing new, but the internet has capitalized on it in fresh ways. For example, the term "clickbait" refers to sensationalist articles published on the internet.

Of course, the twenty-four-hour news cycle also produces its share of sensational stories. Because the media broadcasts news twenty-four hours a day, every second must be filled with a story. However, sometimes there is not much news happening, and sometimes there are no developments to an important story. In both cases, the media must still fill the air time regardless. News networks may be tempted to share a story that is less about news and more about keeping the audience's attention so that the network can generate revenue.

Sensationalism did not start with the twenty-four-hour news cycle, though. Experts on the history of news have found thousands of examples of sensationalism since the advent of newspapers. Joseph Pulitzer is just one example of a respected publisher who printed sensationalist stories. The Pulitzer Prizes, a set of prestigious awards honoring journalism and the arts, are named after the nineteenth-century media giant. However, even Pulitzer published sensational stories in order to sell more newspapers.

Joseph Pulitzer left his mark on American journalism. However, even he published sensationalist news stories.

Turner was named *Time* magazine's "Man of the Year" in 1991. A quarter of a century later, in 2015, Atlanta, Georgia, honored him. CNN is headquartered in Atlanta. A section of Spring Street was renamed Ted Turner Drive.

In 2016, Turner sold his 43,000-acre (17,400-hectare) ranch in Oklahoma to the Osage Nation. He had been practicing environmentally friendly ranching methods there. The sale returned some of the land that the tribe had lived on until 1906. In 1906, the US government broke up the land for individual ownership. *Indian Country Today* reports that Turner wrote a letter to the tribe's chief. "It is my sincere hope that our transaction is the last time this land is ever sold," Turner wrote to Chief Geoffrey M. Standing Bear, "and that the Osage Nation owns this land for all future generations."

Tom Johnson: Calm Under Pressure

Tom Johnson was born in 1941 in Macon, Georgia. His mom inspired him to study and work hard. He credits her with a lot of his success. Johnson followed his mother's advice early in his life. His dad never worked much, was often sick, and had only a third-grade education, so he did not have many opportunities for work. When he was fourteen years old, feeling a responsibility to earn some money for his family, Johnson got a job with the local newspaper. He reported on high school sports, but he soon earned more than just a paycheck: his confidence also grew. He says the first time he saw his byline was the first time he thought he might become someone.

Tom Johnson was publisher of the *Los Angeles Times* when he stood for this portrait.

Johnson graduated from the University of Georgia in 1963. He was a student there when the school desegregated, and he covered the story of the university's first two African American students. He wrote about it for both his school paper and his local newspaper. Johnson calls this a "defining moment" in his life. It was the first time he witnessed racism in person. Not all of the white students accepted their new classmates. Some of Johnson's own fraternity brothers were the people yelling at the new students to leave.

As he took notes on the students' first day, Johnson remembered a lesson from his editor at his hometown newspaper. That advice was to "get it right." The editor meant that the most important job of a journalist was to figure out the truth and then write that. Even though those fraternity brothers had been his friends, Johnson included their names in his articles.

He also invited one of the new students, Charlayne Hunter, to work for the school paper. She was interested in journalism, and Johnson thought the newspaper would be a haven for her. Johnson believed his fellow journalism students would support desegregation. He was wrong. Hunter was bullied so much that she quit the paper. Fortunately, she stuck with journalism. Years later, when Johnson was a leader at CNN, he helped recruit her to be one of the network's foreign correspondents.

White House Confidant

Johnson's first job after college was at the White House. His new wife, Edwina, had heard about a fellowship there and encouraged him to apply. This led to Johnson becoming President Lyndon Johnson's press aide. (Even though they had the same last name, they were not related.) The president trusted Johnson enormously. He was one of the few people allowed into the president's most top-secret meetings. When the president died, Johnson made all the funeral arrangements. He even dressed the president's body before it was placed in the casket.

Publisher of the *Los Angeles Times*

The Chandler family had been a wealthy, powerful family in Los Angeles for generations. They had published the *Los Angeles Times* since 1884. Then Otis Chandler met Johnson, and Johnson made a big impression. In 1977, Chandler named Johnson president and chief operating officer of the *Los Angeles Times*. Three years later, Chandler promoted Johnson to publisher and chief executive officer of the newspaper. Johnson became the first person outside the Chandler family to lead the newspaper. That was 1980, the same year Turner was launching CNN.

Chandler wanted Johnson to make the newspaper garner as much respect as the *New York Times*. Johnson helped the *Los Angeles Times* reach record subscription numbers and record profits. The newspaper also received six Pulitzer Prizes while Johnson was publisher. More than anything, Chandler wanted the *Los Angeles Times* to be known as the most progressive newspaper in the country. This angered the conservative members of Chandler's family, who responded by eventually pushing Johnson out.

Johnson hated losing his job. He had been good at it, and he had believed in the newspaper's mission. This loss bothered him in one other way. He had struggled with depression his whole life. Now, the disease flared up again. "When I was stripped of my job as publisher of the *Los Angeles Times*," he recalls, "it was as though it stripped away who I was, my everything." He sought help. Unfortunately, nothing seemed to work that well. Fortunately, he was about to experience yet another major change in his life, and this one actually helped his depression. He was about to get a new job, with CNN, in a new city, Atlanta. He credits those changes—new city, new work, new doctor, and new medication—with feeling better. Since retiring from CNN in 2001, Johnson has devoted himself to supporting increased research on mental illness.

Out of One Fire and into Another

In 1990, Ted Turner called Johnson and asked him, "Would you really become president of CNN?" Johnson told Georgia Public Broadcasting years later that he thought this was a very funny question. Johnson encouraged them both to slow down and make sure he would be right for the job. Eventually, he did accept.

On Johnson's second day working at CNN, the first Gulf War started. It was August 2, 1990. Johnson's first decision as head of CNN helped cement his legacy. He immediately focused on technology. He wanted to be able to have direct, reliable, constant, and fast communication throughout the entire Middle East. However, that would be expensive. He would exceed his budget by $8 million—maybe even as much as $35 million! The tech required was very new, and the media did not budget for such things. Turner told his new president, "You spend whatever you think it takes, pal."

A Famous Pen

In 1991, Mikhail Gorbachev announced he would resign as president of the Soviet Union. In doing so, he would become the last president of the USSR. The Union of Soviet Socialist Republics would no longer exist. Instead, all the republics would become separate, independent countries.

Johnson flew to Moscow to try to get the final interview with the final leader of the USSR. He joined Gorbachev in the room where he would resign. The documents in front of Gorbachev would transfer power of the new Russia to Boris Yeltsin. They would also officially dissolve the USSR. Television cameras were ready to film Gorbachev signing the historic documents.

Less than thirty seconds to air, Gorbachev picked up his pen to test it. It didn't work. He looked to his aide. His aide did not have an extra pen. Johnson reached in his pocket. He pulled out his pen, a fancy one made by the Mont Blanc company. "Is it American?" Gorbachev asked Johnson. Johnson said the pen was not. "In that case, I'll use it," Gorbachev said. According to Johnson, Gorbachev did not want to use an American-made pen to dissolve the Soviet Union because the United States and the USSR had been engaged in the Cold War for decades and were fierce enemies. Gorbachev signed the documents—and then he put Johnson's pen in his pocket. The pen had been a birthday present from Johnson's wife, so he asked for it back. (He later donated it to the Newseum museum in Washington, DC.)

Johnson recounted this story in an interview with Georgia Public Broadcasting. Upon hearing it, Johnson's interviewer remarked, "That is a wonderful story," to which Johnson responded, "It has the added benefit of truth." To Johnson, truth is the hallmark of a story well told.

CNN's "Boys of Baghdad"

When Operation Desert Storm started in January 1991, only three Western journalists managed to report out to the world from Baghdad, Iraq. Desert Storm was the United States–led combat mission to push the Iraqi military out of Kuwait. The reporters, Bernard Shaw, Peter Arnett, and John Holliman, worked for CNN. This story would help to define the network and those reporters' careers. They were nicknamed the Boys of Baghdad.

Bernard Shaw

Bernard Shaw had always wanted to report on the world's stories. In 1943, when he was three years old, he was in an accelerated reading program in the Carter School on the South Side of Chicago. He fell asleep in that class once, and his teacher scolded him. "She towered over me," Shaw recalls, "and she said, young man, God has given you a gift and you will not waste it in my classroom." She was right.

In high school, Shaw sneaked into news conferences happening near his home. He also called reporters whose stories he read. He asked them for tips and advice. Shaw then entered the US Marines and was stationed in Hawaii. Walter Cronkite was anchor of the CBS *Evening News* then. When Cronkite visited Hawaii, Shaw left him tons of messages, asking to meet. Shaw finally connected with the anchor in his hotel lobby and asked him questions

CNN anchor Bernard Shaw attends the ACE Awards not long after his historic Baghdad coverage.

about having a career in journalism. "He was the most persistent guy I've ever met in my life," Cronkite told the *Washington Post* years later. "I was going to give him five begrudging minutes and ended up talking to him for a half hour. He was just determined to be a journalist."

Shaw got more than just advice from that conversation. A decade later, he had a degree in history from the University of Illinois at Chicago and a few years of experience reporting for the radio. He was ready for a bigger role in journalism. Cronkite agreed. He helped Shaw get a job at CBS, where Shaw would be a political reporter from 1971 to 1977. He then took a job with ABC as a Latin America correspondent from 1977 to 1979.

In 1980, Ted Turner offered Shaw an anchor job at "a network that didn't exist." Shaw was hesitant, but his wife saw beyond what many called "a harebrained scheme." She told Shaw that he needed to take the job just in case CNN did succeed.

Shaw's work at CNN, including his work reporting from Iraq, earned him a lot of praise. At the time, famous interviewer Larry King called him a "folk hero." Still, Shaw's focus remained elsewhere.

"So we did extremely well on that story—so what?" he told the *Washington Post* in January 1991, soon after the outbreak of the war. "Next week we still have to be responsible and accurate and on top of the news. If you sit around fondling the clips, you're going to be in trouble. This war's going to be history one day." Shaw meant that maintaining a high professional standard of journalism from day to day was more important than the success of any one story. He sometimes feared for his life while reporting from Iraq, but he dismissed those fears by saying to himself, "If you're going to die, die doing what you love to do."

Shaw has always placed an emphasis on helping others. "I wasn't born doing this," he says of his career. "So many hands, helping hands, are on my shoulders; I can't count them. So I have a responsibility to pass it on."

Peter Arnett

Peter Arnett is a hero to many in his native New Zealand. In 1966, he became the first journalist from that country to win a Pulitzer Prize. He won the award for investigative reporting on the Vietnam War as a journalist for the Associated Press (AP). As of 2017, he was still the only New Zealander to have won the Pulitzer.

Winning the Pulitzer was the glitzy conclusion to the gutsy first chapter of his journalism career. Arnett got his first reporting job when he was seventeen years old, in 1951. He wrote headlines for his local newspaper. Finally, an editor told him to go outside and write one paragraph about the beautiful weather. The next day, Arnett opened the newspaper to read his first published article. The paragraph was different from what he had written, though. He later learned that his article had been heavily edited. Arnett says he learned an important lesson from that experience: "Write it hard, and tight. Forget the fluff."

This advice helped Arnett as he began his career in war reporting. When he was twenty-six years old, he was assigned to cover Southeast Asia for the Associated Press. He went to the country of Laos, where a violent political coup was underway.

The technology he had to work with then was different from what he would have to work with during his Gulf War coverage for CNN. After he typed his story on a typewriter, he had to get it out to the world. There was no communication from Laos. He had to cross the Mekong River into Thailand; however, all the bridges were closed. There were no boats running.

Undeterred, Arnett stripped down to just his pants. He put his passport, twenty ten-dollar bills, and the one

Peter Arnett pauses for a photo after reporting from the Gulf War in 1991.

copy of his article between his teeth. He stepped into the river and swam across. He then hitchhiked into the closest town with a telegraph office. He gave the telegraph operator half of his money to send the story to his publisher. Arnett swam back to Laos and would make the trip again—more than once. Sometimes he carried more than just his own work. Sometimes he carried multiple pages of typed articles and several rolls of film.

CNN hired Arnett and sent him to the Middle East. Arnett's voice was one people at home heard when they turned on the news the night the Gulf War started. Fellow journalist Mike McRoberts says Arnett's 1991 reporting from Baghdad "chang[ed] conflict journalism forever." According to McRoberts, "Once Peter and CNN had done it, that was it. The door was open. That became the new go-to position in a war."

John Holliman

John Holliman "begged his bosses" at CNN to be assigned to Baghdad, the *Washington Post* reported in 1991. He explained his reasoning to the *Post*: "You can stay [in Washington] and cover some Post Office hearing on [Capitol] Hill or you can go to the story of the decade. If you're a reporter, what could be better than to be there to cover a war?"

The other two Boys of Baghdad appreciated his skills. "When the bombing started, we immediately lost power, so we thought we wouldn't be able to broadcast," Peter Arnett told CNN in 1998. Holliman was able to fix their equipment. "He's the one who made that first broadcast possible. He had a real knowledge of broadcasting," Arnett recalled.

John Holliman reports from the Baghdad war zone in 1991.

When Holliman was sent to Baghdad, he was forty-two years old. He and his wife were living a relatively quiet life. They raised English sheep dogs on a farm outside of Washington, DC. This closeness to the nation's capital allowed Holliman to also work as a journalist.

After earning a degree in journalism from the University of Georgia, he took jobs in radio journalism in Georgia and then in Washington, DC. Holliman worked the agriculture beat for many years for the AP. He reported on food production for the Associated Press Radio Network,

AP's broadcast wire, and its national newspaper wire during the second half of the 1970s. Holliman received the 1976 Peabody Award for his documentary *The Garden Plot: Food as a Weapon in International Diplomacy*. He became so knowledgeable in agriculture that he also taught at the graduate school of the US Department of Agriculture.

Holliman had joined CNN in 1980 as the network's farm reporter. His assignments had changed by the end of the decade. In 1989, he covered the student demonstrations in China, known in the West as Tiananmen Square. That same year, he covered Hurricane Hugo when it hit the coast of North and South Carolina.

Holliman died in September 1998 in a car crash. At the time, he was a national correspondent for CNN based in Atlanta, Georgia. He was the lead reporter for NASA's Pathfinder mission to Mars in the summer of 1997. Had he lived, he was going to co-anchor, with Walter Cronkite, John Glenn's return to space in October 1998. After Holliman's death, Tom Johnson told CNN, "I expect he'll be up there watching the mission from the heavens, probably shouting, 'Holy cow, what a sight!'"

Rupert Murdoch: "The Dirty Digger"

Like his rival, CNN's Ted Turner, Rupert Murdoch of Fox News has had his own share of nicknames. The Dirty Digger is one that has been used often.

Murdoch was born in 1931 in Melbourne, Australia. His family was part of the Australian aristocracy. The Murdochs were wealthy and respected. They loved Australia so much that they hated the "old country," the United Kingdom. (Australia is part of the Commonwealth of Nations. It retains ties to the United Kingdom.)

Maury Povich: Infotainment's Early Host

Infotainment is a cousin to sensationalism. The word is a portmanteau, combining the sounds and meanings of two other words. Infotainment is media that offers information ("info-") and entertainment ("-tainment"). As with sensationalism, many people think the twenty-four-hour news cycle created infotainment. In this case, they're correct. The only way to keep an audience's attention all day every day was to offer entertainment along with the information.

Maury Povich smiles in 1990, as his career takes off.

Maury Povich was born in 1939 in Washington, DC. He graduated from the University of Pennsylvania in 1962 with a degree in television journalism. He became famous when Rupert Murdoch, who founded Fox News, hired him to host *A Current Affair* in 1986. That television show was an early example of infotainment. Povich discussed "the increasingly 'blurred' distinction between news and entertainment" when he spoke at his alma mater in 1997. The *Daily Pennsylvanian*, the college newspaper, reported on his speech.

Povich said that the media has always sold "flashy" stories. The many years of major world events in the 1950s through the 1960s may have left little room for anything other than serious headlines. Journalists delivered news of the Cuban Missile Crisis, the Vietnam War, the civil rights movement, the women's rights movement, and the deaths of President John F. Kennedy and civil rights leader Martin Luther King Jr. This made people associate reporters with hard-hitting and quality stories. They forgot that some "light" stories were published too.

Then, Povich said, there was "a shift in network priorities" during the 1970s and 1980s, "decades characterized by condensed news stories, celebrity gossip and 'infotainment.'" Povich was part of that wave of journalism. One University of Pennsylvania student even called him a "founding father" of the field.

Murdoch's father was at one time "the biggest name in Australian journalism," according to the *Guardian*. However, when he died, he left his son only one small newspaper, the *Adelaide Evening News*.

Murdoch attended Oxford University in England. According to the *Guardian*, "Many people saw Murdoch even then pretty much as he saw himself—a rebel and an outsider from the start." As a result, he returned to Australia. Within fifteen years, he had made his own name in media by buying up failing newspapers and turning them around.

Murdoch even bought a British newspaper, the *News of the World*. Its first big story under his ownership was the "classic tabloid fare" he liked to publish. It was "anti-establishment with a decidedly racy twist and a great commercial opportunity," says the *Guardian*. To Murdoch, the business opportunity was most important. He had learned a lesson when his father died: Public reputation means nothing after you pass away. What lasts after death is the legacy of what you own. Murdoch made the decision to make money and have control. However, according to the *Guardian*, "the liberal establishment reacted with fury" to Murdoch's first *News of the World* story. "All they could see was an old story rehashed purely for commercial gain by a grasping colonial for whom no gutter was too deep." He became the Dirty Digger.

Undeterred, Murdoch bought his first US newspaper in 1973. He then founded the national tabloid newspaper the *Star*. In 1985, he moved into television. He purchased 20th Century Fox Film Corporation. Murdoch became known for expressing his conservative political and social views through his media holdings, including the Fox News Channel, which was launched in 1996.

The Intersection of Storytellers and Their Stories

The storytellers of television news aim to communicate information, share the details of events happening, and tell the stories their audiences need and want to hear. Sometimes, there are stories that capture the imagination of both journalists and the public. The next chapter talks about several such major news events that changed journalism—and the world.

On January 28, 1986, the explosion of the *Challenger* space shuttle was broadcast live.

The Headlines That Kept People Watching

There are many storytellers in the history of the twenty-four-hour news cycle. There are also many critical stories that changed the face of the industry. This chapter covers three such stories that shaped both the news and the world. These stories were integral in the creation of the twenty-four-hour news cycle. Once that cycle had taken hold, other networks—most notably Fox News—entered the fray.

First, CNN's coverage of the *Challenger* space shuttle tragedy in 1986 introduced many people to the network. Second, in 1991, CNN reported live from Baghdad, Iraq, the moment US bombs started falling on the capital city during Operation Desert Storm. This showed the public they could expect instantaneous news coverage of events happening in even the most remote or unstable parts of the world. Third, CNN's continuous reporting on the O. J. Simpson arrest and murder trial in 1994 and 1995 taught people that they could turn on their televisions at any time, day or night, and watch a news story unfolding in real time.

However, by the end of the 1990s, CNN was not the only network on air reporting the news at all hours of the day and night. Fox News, too, made a name for itself when it became the only network to cover a scandal related to President Bill Clinton's reelection campaign. These stories clearly demonstrate how twenty-four-hour news became what it is today.

The *Challenger* Shuttle Disaster

In the twenty-first century, people expect to see historic (and not so historic) events as they happen or moments later. Professional media organizations have kept up with technology, so they are always reporting. Also, even people who are not journalists are reporting on the news. Anyone with a smartphone can record an event. As soon as they connect to the internet, they can upload the recording. The entire world can witness even a very local event recorded by a passerby.

In 1986, the world was a very different place. It was common not to learn about an event until hours after it happened. People did not carry cameras in their pockets. People who missed the news or wanted to learn more had to wait for their newspaper to arrive the next day.

Considering these limitations, it was amazing that a television network broadcast the NASA space shuttle *Challenger* tearing apart in the skies over Florida on January 28, 1986. NASA broadcast the launch in school classrooms because there was a teacher on the shuttle. However, CNN was the only network that broadcast the

The *Challenger* crew included high school teacher Christa McAuliffe (*back row, second from the left*).

full shuttle launch as it happened to the general public, so it was the only network to show the explosion as it happened.

Covering a Tragedy

There was one more twist to the day. CNN's promotions department just happened to be filming its own newsroom that day. Therefore, there is also footage of a newsroom reacting to a major news event happening in the moment. The cameras captured a space busy with reporters, editors, producers, and crew working. The control room, anchor desk, and newsroom were all beside each other. One moment, Bob Furnad, a CNN executive, shouts for everyone to shut up. Another moment, someone is talking about how the president's State of the Union address, which had been scheduled for that night, may be canceled. There may be plans to run a show on the astronauts instead. One of the CNN staff members says into the camera that the network was "a long way from history but responsible for making sure we covered it." CNN was not the focus of the day, but they did play an important role. They brought the story to the world as it happened.

That moment was CNN's "coming of age," Steve Stahl told the network for a thirty-year anniversary article. In 1986, he was a videotape operator for CNN. "After this coverage, I rarely had to explain to people what CNN was."

Because CNN was young, much of its staff was also new. "Working with a young staff with limited experience in putting live, breaking news on the air was amazing," Furnad told CNN years later.

Even staff experienced with reporting the news were stunned by the unexpected events. John Zarrella was the CNN correspondent at Kennedy Space Center. His recollections of the experience are documented in a blog post for CNN. "I was expecting it to be routine, like the launches I had covered in the past," he says. Then, about a minute after the shuttled launched, something strange happened: "From where I was standing, you could see a cloud of smoke and then what looked like fireworks shooting out from the cloud," Zarrella writes. It was so out of the ordinary that at first none of the journalists standing by the countdown clock understood what it

The media learns more information about the *Challenger*'s deadly failed takeoff.

meant. "We just looked at each other with puzzled faces as we waited for the orbiter to appear from behind the cloud," Zarrella remembers.

Zarrella ran to Steve Sonnenblick, the CNN photographer shooting live from the launch pad. Zarrella knew Sonnenblick would have seen clearly what happened because he was looking through his zoom lens. Sonnenblick confirmed that the shuttle looked to him like it had exploded.

Zarrella ran next to the space center, which was in "total chaos," he writes. "Reporters were screaming at the NASA public affairs officers, demanding that they be taken out to the space shuttle landing strip ... The

NASA folks were screaming back that no one was going anywhere until they had a better understanding of what had happened. At times you really felt like fistfights were going to break out."

Holding Back Emotions

During a major news event, emotions run high among producers, reporters, and photographers. Everyone wants to do a good job covering the story. The story is always changing, however. Facts must always be double-checked for accuracy. Details must constantly be updated. There are also a lot of moving parts behind the scenes in the newsroom, especially since technology can be complicated, producers and reporters can have different visions, and viewers can be demanding.

However, as they are reporting, journalists must keep their personal emotions about an event in check. This doesn't mean that journalists don't feel the effects of the tragedies they cover. Zarrella says that witnessing the horror of the *Challenger* explosion affected him for a long time afterward. "The nightmares I had of space shuttles exploding finally ended, but it took several years."

In the video of the CNN newsroom from that day, one of the network staff members explains what it felt like—or did not feel like—to cover a tragedy: "My job began just at the time that this tragic accident occurred, and I was not permitted to have emotional feelings about it. I will have those later. I had to represent this network in doing the things that it is expected to do."

That can be a heavy burden to carry in a twenty-four-hour news cycle. The news coverage never stops, so there are few breaks for media professionals. As professionals, reporters are supposed to simply observe an event and share the facts of what happened. As human beings, they will react emotionally to events. Their job requires them to be "on" all the time and objectively share black-and-white details that do not include their subjective perspective. However, their nature requires some time to process events and form their own private opinions.

The First Gulf War

Coverage of the *Challenger* explosion gave the fledgling network some name recognition and credibility, yet the first Gulf War is the event that made CNN famous. CNN's reporting of the war won a National Headliner Award, the George Foster Peabody Award, and a Golden Microphone Award.

Timeline of Conflict

In May 1990, Saddam Hussein, president of Iraq, accused neighboring countries Kuwait and the United Arab Emirates of "economic warfare." Two months later, in July, Iraq accused Kuwait of stealing oil from an oil field on the border between the two countries. On August 2, Iraq's military invaded Kuwait. Iraqi troops also lined up along the border with Saudi Arabia.

Saudi Arabia requested help from the United States, and the United States sent troops. In September, the United Kingdom and France also sent troops. On December 17, the United Nations told Iraq that it needed to leave Kuwait by January 15, 1991.

On January 12, the US Congress gave President George H. W. Bush the authority to go to war against Iraq. Days

American military members watch oil well fires in Iraq. The Gulf War was a turning point in television news.

later, the war started. It was 2:30 a.m. on January 17 in Baghdad, the capital of Iraq. Across the United States, it was still January 16, and many people were ending their workdays or getting ready for dinner.

Arriving in Baghdad

Before Operation Desert Storm started, people still hoped President Hussein would listen to the United Nations and withdraw his troops from Kuwait. CNN wanted an interview with Hussein on January 15, the deadline for withdrawal. CNN anchor Bernard Shaw flew to Iraq to interview him. Meanwhile, CNN reporter Peter Arnett, normally stationed in Jerusalem, Israel, was allowed to go to Baghdad. CNN reporter John Holliman joined them. CNN producer Robert Wiener was there too. They stayed together in the Al-Rasheed Hotel in the capital city of Baghdad.

Hussein did not go to the interview. Instead, Shaw talked with another Iraqi official. That man told the reporter that Hussein planned to ignore the United Nations' request that he withdraw Iraqi troops from Kuwait. Shaw had a feeling this would start a war. So did the rest of world, once they heard the news.

From Baghdad, Shaw reported on Hussein's plans. Immediately, he got a call from CNN headquarters in Atlanta. "There was all this screaming and confusion," Shaw told the *Washington Post* about a week later. Because of his news report, the stock market had gone down forty-seven points. This was scary to people. The drop indicated that everyone was uncertain what the future would hold—but they suspected the situation in Iraq would worsen.

Shaw's producer back in the United States asked the anchor to broadcast a follow-up report. He asked him to "clarify" what he had reported. By "clarify," the producer meant "soften." In other words, Shaw was supposed to calm CNN viewers down and tell them everything would be OK. Shaw refused. "I said, 'Wait a minute. I don't have to clarify a damn thing ... I will repeat what I reported and I will repeat it very slowly.'"

Shaw told NPR decades later, "One of the things I strove for was to be able to control my emotions in the midst of hell breaking out. And I personally feel that I passed my stringent test for that in Baghdad ... It would be a disservice to the consumers of news—be they readers, listeners or viewers—for me to become emotional and to get carried away."

After that report, Shaw thought his work in Iraq was done. He told viewers on the afternoon of Wednesday, January 16, 1991, "I'm going to be wheels-up out of here tomorrow, and I leave Baghdad very disappointed that I have not accomplished the mission that I had."

Hours later, Shaw was still in Iraq, bombs were exploding all around him, and he was trying to make an emergency connection to CNN.

The First Broadcast from Baghdad

Georgia Public Broadcasting (GPB) calls the night US bombs started falling on Baghdad a "remarkable evening in television." It was unique because CNN prioritized technology like no other network did, or could.

The four members of the CNN staff had a four-wire phone hookup. This is a private phone line that does not rely on the regular phone system. It also consists of two pairs of telephone lines instead of one, which means sets

The Evolution of Tech in the Newsroom

In the 1980s, technology that once existed only in sci-fi stories was becoming real. Some of this exciting technology changed the newsroom forever.

The computer became an important tool for reporters and producers. Its connection to science fiction was clear in so many ways. William Shatner, who played Captain Kirk on the television series *Star Trek*, even advertised the Commodore personal computer in 1980. In 1981, the 3.5-inch (9 cm) floppy disk was introduced to the market. This invention allowed journalists to save stories and carry them with them. In many word-processing programs, an icon that looks like a floppy disk is still used to indicate "save." In 1982, *Time* magazine named not a "Man of the Year" but a "Machine of the Year": the personal computer. The magazine's publisher, John A. Meyers, wrote that no person "symbolized the past year more richly, or will be viewed by history as more significant, than a machine: the computer." The magazine's lead writer on the "Machine of the Year" wrote the story on a typewriter. Meyers said the magazine's newsroom would replace its typewriters with computers by 1983.

Satellite newsgathering trucks also created new possibilities. These trucks allowed journalists to travel many miles from their news studio to cover a story. They could then send, or beam, their reports back to their home stations. According to an article in the *Balance*, "Stations looked for any reason to use this equipment, even driving hundreds of miles to cover hurricanes that didn't threaten their local coverage area."

The United Press International's New York City newsroom in 1986 flaunts "new" technology.

of callers and receivers can both listen and speak with each other at the same time. Bombs fell all around the CNN reporters. They were in a war zone. Still, because of the four-wire, their communication signal got through. In fact, at one point, NBC news anchor Tom Brokaw interviewed Shaw. That was as close as any of the "big three" networks would come to covering the war so completely and so immediately.

The other networks also had four-wire technology. If the young CNN could afford it, the more established networks certainly could. A four-wire cost only $15,000 a month in 1991 (equal to about $28,000 in 2018), which was nothing compared with the millions spent on other technology. However, only CNN was granted approval by the Iraqi government to use the four-wire. According to one CNN source who spoke with the *Los Angeles Times*, it was the perseverance of the CNN crew, including Wiener, that made Iraqi officials finally say yes to the network's four-wire. They kept asking for permission until they received it. An NBC source said Iraq gave CNN approval because CNN was Hussein's favorite television network.

For months, CNN had made a name for itself among the other networks as being willing to broadcast photo ops and news from Hussein's administration. Iraqi government and military officials could watch themselves regularly on CNN—not ABC, CBS, or NBC. They saw CNN relaying clips of their newscasters' reports to the world. Therefore, they believed CNN when the network said it was ready and able to give Hussein airtime and an audience with the American public. "The network was, in short," the *New York Times* wrote in 1992, "Baghdad's link to the outside." CNN covering the war was, in that moment, good for both the Iraqi government and CNN. As Wiener said at the time, "We're using them, they're using us."

However, no one knew how long this opportunity would last. While they had the ability to broadcast, CNN's Boys of Baghdad wanted to. Shaw started "screaming" at CNN's headquarters in Atlanta to put him on the air. "This is—something is happening outside," he told the world. "Peter Arnett, join me here. Let's describe to our viewers what we're seeing. The skies over Baghdad have been illuminated. We're seeing bright flashes going off all over the sky."

Back in the United States, the press secretary for President George H. W. Bush called CNN station president Tom Johnson. He told Johnson to get his reporters out of there. It was too dangerous. Johnson thanked him for the call and hung up. Immediately, General Colin Powell, the chairman of the Joint Chiefs of Staff (a group of high-ranking military advisers to the US president), called Johnson. He reiterated that it was too dangerous to have journalists in Baghdad. Powell also said it was jeopardizing his military mission. Johnson again said thanks and disconnected. In the next moment, President Bush himself called. That did it, and now Johnson was really worried. He called Ted Turner to talk over the options. Johnson was beginning to think that maybe he should pull his correspondents out of Baghdad. Turner encouraged him to leave them there.

This led to mixed feelings from the men on the ground. "When every major newspaper pulled out, that was frightening," Shaw told the *Washington Post* later that month. He also felt excitement about the unique opportunity. "We knew we had a responsibility to cover the story even more extensively. Obviously, selfishly, we knew it would enhance the reputation of our network."

The night was, of course, scarier than it was invigorating. Later that night, the reporters' broadcast went silent. Johnson worried he had made a mistake. He feared the hotel where the men were reporting from had been bombed. After a tense time, the signal started again. "They had not died!" Johnson remembered to Georgia Public Broadcasting nearly thirty years later. "Their battery had died."

The risk of being hit by bombs was high. So was the possibility that the Iraqi government or military would shut CNN's broadcast down. "My biggest concern was an Iraqi backlash to what we were doing," Shaw told the *Washington Post*.

Whenever there was a knock at the door to the hotel suite they were broadcasting from, Shaw would run to another room and hide. If hotel security was at the door, and if they took Holliman and Arnett, Shaw could keep broadcasting.

Into the Bomb Shelter

Sixteen and a half hours after the journalists' first report, the Iraqi government ordered CNN to stop broadcasting. The men were moved, along with three hundred other hotel guests, to the hotel's bomb shelter. There had been a rumor that the hotel was a US bombing target. The men hated knowing that they had so much high-tech communications equipment in their room and could not use it, not even to tell people they were safe.

According to the *Washington Post*, Holliman came up with a plan. He told the guards he needed medicine

CNN showed this graphic when Bernard Shaw reported from Baghdad in 1991.

Baghdad, Iraq

Bernard Shaw
CNN Reporting

from the journalists' room. The guards let him leave the bomb shelter for a few minutes. He ran to the four-wire and connected to CNN's offices in Atlanta. "This is Holliman," he whispered. "Tell our families we're okay." The producers asked if they could put him on the air. He said no. It was too risky. He did not have long, and Iraqi officials were monitoring CNN.

Moving Day

The increased censorship by the Iraqi military and government against Western journalists was a problem. The CNN reporters worried they could not do their job. On Friday morning, a day after the US bombing started, Shaw and Holliman decided to leave Baghdad. Arnett stayed behind, just in case.

Their trip out of the capital city was long and dangerous. They were part of a three-car CNN convoy.

They drove for fourteen hours across the western Iraqi desert. Iraqi authorities stopped them fifteen times. Finally, they crossed the border into Jordan. They went to that country's capital city, Amman. That night, Shaw and Holliman connected with Atlanta, and the world, again.

"Making History"

The war in Iraq was complicated and had implications that lasted into the twenty-first century. News coverage of it was also complicated. However, among all the complex answers, and lack of answers, that surround the war, one thing is clear. Twenty-four-hour news not only reported the headlines of the time but made them. At one point during that first night of reporting from the Al-Rasheed, Arnett exclaimed to Shaw and Holliman, "Gentlemen, you and you and I are making history tonight." It would not be the last time CNN made history.

O. J. Simpson: The Slow-Speed Chase

Tom Johnson has said that two people made his career at CNN. One was Saddam Hussein. He was president of Iraq when CNN made history covering the US war with Iraq. The other was O. J. Simpson—professional football player, actor, and accused murderer.

Simpson was born in 1947 in San Francisco, California. He earned fame early in his life. When he was a football player at the University of Southern California, he won the Heisman Trophy, a prestigious award given to one college football player every year. That person is expected to be an outstanding athlete and someone who demonstrates living with integrity.

People watch as O. J. Simpson passes during a slow-speed car chase on June 17, 1994.

After college, Simpson joined the professional football team the Buffalo Bills in 1969. He broke numerous records during his decade playing professional football. He retired from the sport in 1979. He then became an actor in movies and commercials and a commentator for the sports program *Monday Night Football*.

In 1985, Simpson married Nicole Brown. In 1992, she filed for divorce. Two years later, CNN covered a tragedy involving Simpson and Brown Simpson. The network again captured many people's attention and kept them watching their televisions.

Timeline of a Double Murder

On Sunday, June 12, 1994, Brown Simpson, her children, her mother, and friends went to a restaurant in Los Angeles. They returned home after dinner. At 9:15 p.m., they called the restaurant, realizing that Brown Simpson's mother had forgotten her glasses there. Brown Simpson's friend Ron Goldman, a waiter at the restaurant, offered to return the glasses.

At 10:15 p.m., Brown Simpson's neighbors heard a dog barking nonstop from next door. Shortly after midnight, a passerby noticed Brown Simpson and Goldman lying dead just outside her house.

O. J. Simpson was an early suspect in the murders. Later that week, police issued a warrant for his arrest. On Friday, June 17, Simpson's lawyer, Robert Shapiro, went to the house where Simpson had been staying. They told the police he would turn himself in at 11:00 a.m. that day. By noon, he still had not surrendered. The police called Shapiro and told him they now considered Simpson a fugitive. Shapiro said Simpson had left the house with his friend and former football teammate Al Cowlings. The California Highway Patrol issued an all-points bulletin. All police in the state were now looking for Simpson.

They eventually found Cowlings's white Ford Bronco. He was driving while Simpson hid in the back seat. Cowlings and Simpson led the police on a two-hour car chase. Because it was rush hour in Los Angeles, the chase was very slow. Finally, the men surrendered at Simpson's mansion. Simpson was allowed to call his mother, drink a glass of juice, and use the restroom. Police then took him into custody. Cowlings was charged with helping a fugitive.

Watching a Murder Case

The public demonstrated an insatiable interest in the case from the beginning. During the slow-speed car chase, people cheered from overpasses. Many who had been driving pulled over, got out of their cars, and waved. People from across the country called in to KNX-AM news radio to broadcast requests to Simpson that he turn himself in. Simpson was at his mansion for over an hour after the chase. During that time, hundreds of people gathered on his street. They chanted, "Free O. J." They rocked police cars.

Many more people watched on television. Cable and network stations covered the chase and arrests. The sound of the news helicopters over the chase became part of the scene. The coverage dramatically overshadowed the fifth game in the National Basketball Association championship finals, which was taking place at the same time. The *Los Angeles Times* painted a picture in an article the next day: "In downtown bars people watched television sets, once primed for the championship basketball series, now tuned only to the breaking news story. At the Spectrum Club in Santa Monica, exercisers pedaled stationary bikes to TV sets tuned to coverage of O. J. Simpson's temporary disappearance. Downtown streets were deserted."

The Tower Records store in Los Angeles tuned its fifteen television monitors to the Simpson story. "It's paralyzed our business," the store manager told the *Los Angeles Times*. Customers were frozen in the aisles, watching the television sets "in awe."

Part of the reason for the public interest was celebrity. Simpson was famous and popular. The other reason was the news stations reported every little detail, so the story seemed to be changing minute by minute. Viewers thought that if they looked away from their televisions for even a short time, they would miss something. Before the internet, television delivered the fastest, most complete news coverage. Unlike radio, newspapers, and magazines, television offered video and audio. With twenty-four-hour news, television accomplished this as the news happened.

The networks filled in the slow moments with extra, supporting footage of Simpson's life story. "Every move was chronicled on live television," the *Los Angeles Times* said the next day. "Now [Simpson] was reported missing, now feared dead, now alive and headed south on Interstate 5." The car chase was slow, but the news reporting was fast. Television news reported updates almost before the last update had happened: "Before the police could finish announcing that he had disappeared, the drama had shifted back to the scene of the crime," the *Los Angeles Times* explained.

CNN was devoted to covering the news twenty-four hours a day. It talked about Simpson during the chase, the arrest, and the trial. "Just like Saddam Hussein brought us record, record, record audience levels, the O. J. Simpson story brought us off-the-chart audience levels," Tom Johnson told Georgia Public Broadcasting decades later. He said that sometimes CNN wanted to break away from the Simpson trial. Other important events were happening in the world that the network wanted to cover. Every time they did so, people called the network to complain.

The Start of Fox News

With major stories like the *Challenger* explosion, the Gulf War, and the O. J. Simpson trial, CNN helped the twenty-four-hour news cycle to start spinning. After a short time, the network was beholden to that very cycle. There was

Memes: A New Form of Political Cartoons

The internet has created a new type of political cartoon: the political meme. According to a 2016 article in the *Week*, political memes are "any humorous image, video, or text with political content that circulates widely on social media." One popular type of meme is a quote placed over an image. The quote may be from a candidate running for public office. The image may be a still photo from a television show or movie. If the person making the meme does not like the candidate, they may choose an image of a fictional character who is known to lie a lot. They may then choose a real quote from the candidate that they do not believe is true. By putting that quote and that fictional character together, the person who is creating the meme is saying that the political candidate is a liar.

"Online political memes … follow in a long line of political cartoons," the *Week* explains. The goal of news articles and broadcasts is to report fact. The goal of political cartoons is to interpret that fact or use humor and visuals to explain the fact. Memes do this with news too. They also bring two new aspects to political cartooning. One, anyone with access to a computer can make a meme. Two, memes can last in the modern news cycle. The *Week* writes, "With a twenty-four-hour news cycle, it's easy for some stories to get lost, but political memes can have a galvanizing effect, bringing attention to the underlying meaning of comments that might have otherwise been ignored."

no stopping what had been started. The network would continue to adapt. It also would be forced to watch as new players joined in and took the lead at different times. One of those was Fox News.

At 6:00 a.m. on October 7, 1996, Fox News Channel launched to seventeen million households. MSNBC, that year's other new twenty-four-hour network, had an audience of twenty-two million. The reason for this difference was, in essence, the first big story for Fox News.

Time Warner, a cable provider, was required by law to carry a CNN competitor. This is an antitrust idea—that competition benefits consumers. Interestingly, at the same time, CNN's parent company, Turner Broadcasting, was merging with Time Warner. Some considered this a potential conflict of interest that would not benefit the consumer. Ted Turner, CNN's founder, and Rupert Murdoch, the founder of Fox News, had long been involved in a vicious fight that crossed professional as well as personal lines.

Fox had an informal agreement with Time Warner to be CNN's competition with the cable provider. Then, four months before Fox launched, Time Warner decided to carry MSNBC instead. This blocked Fox from much of the New York City metro area. Murdoch already had ties to the New York area. For example, he owned the *New York Post* newspaper. So, when his new television network was kept out of the market, Murdoch threatened to pull the two thousand jobs his empire provided the city, along with the $25 million in yearly revenue it earned for the city.

According to CNN, this led to "one of the most nasty and messiest political feuds in a city known for them." The *Chicago Tribune* called it "the stuff of a made-for-

TV drama." Both the New York State governor, George Pataki, and the New York City mayor, Rudy Giuliani, got involved. They supported Murdoch. Giuliani said he would consider allowing Fox News to broadcast over public-access channels. Fox News filed a lawsuit to prevent Time Warner from merging with Turner Broadcasting. In response, Time Warner went to federal court to get a restraining order. The company wanted to prevent Giuliani from making Fox News available by putting the network on public access. Time Warner's president, Richard Parsons, told the court, "What we have here is the city selecting services that, for whatever reason, the city happens to like and directing those services to be put on." The judge sided with Time Warner. Media law experts said this opened the door for similar disputes around the country. More media companies would lean on politicians to get their way.

The dispute did not end for almost a year. On July 23, 1997, Time Warner agreed to carry Fox News. Time Warner would gain access to Murdoch-owned satellite television systems, and Fox News would have access to 65 percent of Time Warner's network. The first major story that New Yorkers could now watch, which they could not before, was the US Senate hearings on campaign finance abuses. In late 1996, the US Justice Department started investigating President Bill Clinton's reelection campaign for possible illegal activity. Fox was the only network that broadcast the hearings live and in full from July to October 1997.

Serious competition within the twenty-four-hour news cycle had begun.

Fox News

FOX News Network, LLC

3 PEGI 3

5 MILLION
Downloads

4.4 ★★★★☆
117,275

News & Magazines

Similar

INSTALL

Get the day's top news stories from Fox News – Fair & Balanced®!

READ MORE

Fox News started as a response to CNN. Today, it is a popular news source that has evolved with the times.

Television News: Forever Changed

The launch of CNN and the early years of the twenty-four-hour news cycle have affected journalism in many ways. One of the biggest effects was the creation and rise of Fox News.

Fox News

In 1996, both MSNBC and Fox News launched. People thought MSNBC would win the battle of the new networks and be CNN's primary competitor. It had the financial backing of General Electric and Microsoft. It also had the decades-long reputation of NBC, the broadcast channel of parent company NBCUniversal Television Group. Rupert Murdoch and his new network surprised everyone by becoming CNN's real challenger.

Behind the Scenes of the Twenty-Four-Hour News Cycle

The twenty-four-hour news cycle impacts everyone involved in media. Reporters' old way of doing business no longer exists. Even the way media rooms are set up has changed drastically to accommodate nonstop news. There is need for structuring media rooms in new ways that support twenty-four-hour viewership of the newsroom. Because news stations broadcast continuously, their sets must both accommodate staff and look good for viewers.

Everything moves faster in the era of twenty-four-hour news. Reporters are always on a deadline. Because journalists are always working on stories, they may try to interview a source without an appointment. Sources have changed their strategies too. There are even coaches to help political figures and others who are involved in news stories know how to react when they're surprised by a reporter.

In 2016, *Adweek* published a story about the work of event organizers in Des Moines, Iowa, who prepared the Microsoft Media Center for the Iowa Caucus for the 2016 US presidential election. Two thousand press people from five hundred media outlets covered the news around the clock in that space. Television audiences could watch everything that unfolded there, often in real time. This meant things had to look nice. For example, the event organizers used 0.5 miles (0.8 km) of carpet and 800 feet (244 meter) of draperies. They also used

Sharp Fighting Begins Along the River Drina on the Bosnian Frontier.

COUNTER INVASION PLAN

Montenegrin and Serb Armies to Invade Bosnia and Start a Rebellion There.

GREY'S PEACE PLAN FAILS

Kaiser Declines to Join in Conference to Exert Pressure on Austrian Ally.

BUT REPLY IS CONCILIATORY

And London Still Has Faith That His Influence Will Avert

Donald Trump speaks after the 2016 Iowa Caucus. Preparing such events to be camera-ready is a massive undertaking.

1,000 feet (305 m) of moveable sections of wall to divide the space into different television news "sets." Meanwhile, 5 miles (8 km) of cable snaked through the space. Pyramids of outlets, powramids, made plugging in easier. IT staff had to be there twenty-four hours a day in case of emergencies.

Roger Ailes

Rupert Murdoch founded Fox News, but Roger Ailes became the recognized face of the channel. After his death in May 2017, even those who disagreed with his conservative politics recognized his importance in media. David Axelrod, chief strategist for Barack Obama's presidential campaigns, tweeted, "The impact of Roger Ailes on American politics & media was indisputable." In February 1996, Murdoch hired Ailes to run Fox News.

He stayed with Fox for its first two decades, leading it to become a powerful conservative news network. In

Roger Ailes, then the Fox News chair and CEO, speaks at the 2006 Summer Television Critics Association Press Tour.

2016, he resigned because of accusations that he had allowed and even participated in sexual harassment at work. His last job was as adviser to the Donald Trump presidential campaign.

The Invasion of Afghanistan: Fox's War

On September 11, 2001, terrorists attacked the United States. On October 7, 2001, US and British military forces invaded Afghanistan, where Osama bin Laden was in hiding. Bin Laden was behind the 9/11 attacks, and the Afghani government would not agree to hand him over to US forces. Within two years, there were ten thousand US troops in Afghanistan. Within seven years, there were thirty-one thousand US troops in the country. By December 1, 2009, eight years after the United States entered Afghanistan, there were seventy-one thousand US troops there.

Back on the home front, in the United States, twenty-four-hour news networks battled for audiences. After the US invasion of Afghanistan, Fox News took the ratings lead over CNN. The first Gulf War solidified CNN's twenty-four-hour-news fame. The fighting in Afghanistan did the same for CNN's main rival. According to the *New York Times*, Fox's average audience in late 2001 was 43 percent larger than it was in late 2000. CNN was in nine million more households than Fox was, but Fox often had a bigger audience than CNN.

According to the *New York Times* in 2001, "The journalistic legacy of this war would seem to be a debate over what role journalism should play at a time of war." Fox News "pushed television news where it has never gone before: to unabashed and vehement support of

American soldiers board a Chinook helicopter in Afghanistan in 2001. Coverage of the war in Afghanistan established Fox News as a ratings powerhouse.

A Fox News correspondent interviews a US soldier in Afghanistan in 2002.

a war effort, carried in tough-guy declarations often expressing thirst for revenge."

David Westin, the president of ABC News, told the *New York Times* that he supported neutrality in news. "The American people right now need at least some sources for their news where they believe we're trying to get it right, plain and simply, rather than because it fits with any advocacy we have."

Roger Ailes, the Fox News chairman, told the *New York Times* that people simply cannot be objective about terrorism. The old journalistic rule that reporters share the facts of a story without including their opinions could not apply, in his view. He said that if his support of subjective journalism made him "a bad guy, tough luck." That did not matter to him. As he said, "I'm still getting the ratings."

The CNN Effect

The media has always played a role in politics and social change. However, some experts think the twenty-four-hour news cycle has done more to effect change than other journalism eras. They refer to this as the "CNN effect," named after the network that is often considered the founding media organization of the twenty-four-hour news cycle. This theory says that the depth, speed, and extent of the twenty-four-hour news cycle give the media more power. The CNN effect is often used when discussing the relationship between the media and political events. However, it can happen in many arenas. For example, Bernard Kouchner, the first United Nations governor of Kosovo, has said, "Where there is no camera, there is no humanitarian intervention."

Some experts think the CNN effect "is not clear-cut." According to Indiana University law professor Fred H. Cate, "The relationship between press coverage and humanitarian relief activities is complex." For Cate, "The power of media images to motivate action has been exaggerated."

However, Cate also has written that the CNN effect is not to be ignored. One way that he sees the modern media as having a huge effect is that relief organizations fight for the attention of journalists. Whether or not media attention leads to political change or social action, many relief organizations think it does. They believe that if they emphasize the negative, the sad, or the frustrating, they will get more publicity and then more support. According to Cate, "Just as the power of the press to prompt public and government responses to humanitarian emergencies is not as great as once thought, the capacity of relief organizations to misinform and to dull public attention is very considerable." To combat this, Cate has urged organizations "to adopt standards for handling communications" with the press. Some organizations have adopted this more restrained approach. For example, in 1994, some of the world's largest humanitarian groups joined together in developing a code of conduct. They agreed to recognize victims of disasters and emergencies as "dignified human beings, not hopeless objects" when they talk to the media.

Looping and Regrouping

Thanks in part to the twenty-four-hour news cycle, the twenty-first century has an "obsession" with watching replays of major events, particularly disasters. We also have "new rituals of public grief on social media," says the *Washington Post*. In 1986, the *Post*'s television critic, Tom Shales, wrote his observations of the television news coverage of the space shuttle *Challenger* tragedy. In his article, which the newspaper reprinted in 2016, he noted people's reliance on rewatching footage of the tragedy.

Shales's first line was, "We may not be able to believe that something truly terrible has happened anymore unless we see it six or seven times on television." He said he first realized the way we process news in 1981. President Ronald Reagan had been shot and almost died. The twenty-four-hour news cycle was just being born. The networks replayed footage of the Reagan shooting until the event "penetrated the national consciousness, rising in impact with each replay until, inevitably, it

A mother and daughter watch coverage of the *Challenger* disaster in 1986.

reached a point of diminishing returns," Shales wrote. Five years later, in 1986, the television networks also offered "marathon coverage" of the *Challenger* tragedy. Finally, "belief takes over," Shales wrote—but only after the twentieth replay.

Shales took comfort in more than just seeing footage of the event repeatedly. He also appreciated what happened between the replays. According to that television critic, during crises, anchors "aren't there just to impart or repeat information; they become, in a sense, national hand holders, figures of supportive strength." Others consider that a negative. NPR's David Folkenflik, for example, says the filler between updates on big stories often means "pulpy, quasi-tabloid, quasi-celebrity news; anything that's sort of waiting for the next great crisis." Shales, however, appreciated the networks' extra material during the *Challenger* coverage. He found it helpful for viewers. For example, NBC interviewed a child psychologist. Many children had watched the *Challenger* tragedy, and many may have needed help understanding their emotions. ABC asked a former astronaut to explain slow-motion replays of the shuttle's destruction. CBS anchor Dan Rather read a poem and, Shales wrote, "achieved the kind of common-man eloquence that makes him not only a valued source of information at a time like this, but a valued companion, someone of authority and yet camaraderie."

The CNN effect is a term that is often used in a negative way. At the time of the *Challenger* disaster, Shales might have used it positively. He said it was quite possible that the White House had watched the twenty-four-hour news cycle on the *Challenger* disaster. And if the president had watched, that may have been why he canceled that night's scheduled State of the Union address. Why, Shales seemed to wonder, would that be a bad thing? It could be seen as a good thing that the president would have access to the mood of the country.

The Twenty-Four-Hour Internet

In the nineteenth century, the second telegram ever sent asked its recipient for the news. Samuel Morse, the inventor of the telegraph, was wondering what was happening far away from him. In other words, he wondered what he was missing. More than 150 years later, the twenty-four-hour news cycle and the internet named this condition the "fear of missing out" (FOMO). The question that CNN and other twenty-four-hour news pioneers sought to answer is still being asked.

In 2012, the *New York Times* wrote a story about Joe Weisenthal, then the lead financial blogger for *Business Insider*. The first tweet he would write every morning after waking up was "What'd I miss?" Financial blogging, the article suggested, was a field dominated by people who "work long hours and comment on every new development." At the time of the profile, over a typical sixteen-hour workday, Weisenthal would write fifteen posts, manage a dozen other reporters, and hold conversations with some of his 19,000 Twitter followers. (Today he has more than 140,000 followers.) He has tweeted photos of himself working at night. He has used the hashtag #FridayNightAloneAtHomeReadingWallStreetResearch. In other words, he was like a one-person twenty-four-hour news team.

Also like a twenty-four-hour news station, Weisenthal produced strong and not-so-strong work each day. "Some of what he writes is air and sugar. Some of it is wrong or incomplete or misleading," the *Times* article said. When you have to fill every moment of every day with information, you will not be at your best all the time. Even with that inconsistency, Weisenthal still succeeded at his job, over all—just like CNN, Fox News, MSNBC, and other strong twenty-four-hour news networks do. "He delivers jolts of sharp, original insight often enough to hold the attention of a high-powered audience" including economists and Wall Street hedge-fund managers and investors, the *New York Times* article explained.

"To me, this kind of journalism, it's fun," Weisenthal told the newspaper. "It's kind of like a game, taking this stuff and making it public and continuing to collapse the gap with what the pros have access to."

Financial blogger Joe Weisenthal (*left*) attends the B5 Media Launch Party in 2010. Weisenthal has leveraged Twitter as a news platform.

CNN did not lead to the internet—far from it. Neither did the telegraph before it. However, cable news networks opened the space for people to believe in a new kind of journalism. With each development in reporting, the public came to expect more from media organizations. This, in turn, led to more developments in reporting.

What's Next?

Advances in satellite technology mean that "hundreds of satellite news channels create worldwide 'information routes,'" according to the *Times Higher Education*. Now, "a globalized, 'networked' public is seeking new spaces of deliberation." These include Twitter and YouTube.

In a 2014 article, the *Guardian* asks, "Have the twenty-four-hour TV news channels had their day?" In answering, the newspaper fast-forwards from CNN's coverage of Operation Desert Storm in 1991 to the internet age. The article suggests that twenty-four-hour news has been redefined by the internet. In the late twentieth century, we needed television news. Broadcast, cable, or satellite—it did not matter. Once the internet became mainstream, in much of the world, twenty-four-hour news took on a whole new meaning. "Cable news established the twenty-four-hour news habit," the *Guardian* argues, "but today social media and mobile phones fulfill the instant news needs of consumers better than any TV channel can."

The *Guardian* suggests that television news should combine with the internet. It would, after all, save money. The infrastructure needed to support a twenty-four-hour news channel is considerable. It requires studio space and always-open satellite links and transponders. It requires enough anchors, reporters, and behind-the-scenes team members like producers, camera crews, and editors.

This combining of media would also allow for all the positives of a twenty-four-hour news cycle without many of the negatives. Newsgathering has become a business to feed itself, the *Guardian* suggests. When a network has

An Early Award for Twenty-Four-Hour News

Television is most often associated with the twenty-four-hour news cycle. This is because the idea of round-the-clock news coverage started with television in the 1980s. However, television was not the only medium for that kind of reporting. The old medium of radio continued to be important to audiences.

On February 4, 1984, the worst snowstorm in forty years blew into the Red River valley, which covers parts of Minnesota and North Dakota and also stretches into the provinces of Manitoba and Saskatchewan in Canada. Thousands of people were trapped by the heavy and sudden blizzard.

KFGO Radio in Fargo, North Dakota, covered the whole storm without stopping. Reporters were on the air for twenty-four hours. They gave updates on the storm and cleanup. They offered travel tips. They also made suggestions on staying safe in the dangerous weather conditions. They opened the phone lines to the radio station. People could call in to broadcast messages to friends and family who were missing in the storm. Many of the missing were people who had been driving when the storm hit. Since this was before cell phones, people at home hoped their radio messages would reach their loved ones trapped in their cars.

Decades after their award-winning coverage of a 1984 snowstorm, radio station KFGO is still on the air.

KFGO received a Peabody Award, a major award for radio and television, for its "extraordinary emergency coverage." The award's judges praised the radio station staff for their "commitment, compassion, and dedication." After all, that's what reporting the news is all about.

to fill twenty-four hours of every day, its job is not just to report the news but to act as though there is news to report. The network leaves a camera trained on an empty courtroom, for example, waiting for a trial to start. Or a correspondent rehashes details just to fill air time until something new happens. In a telling example, a BBC News reporter once said to the viewers at home, "Plenty more to come, none of it news. But that won't stop us."

By working more with the internet, networks could also focus on news that different target markets care about. With television technology only, a network is working with one channel. That means that whatever story it chooses to follow, all viewers around the world will watch only that—unless they change the channel.

The Legacy of Twenty-Four-Hour News

David Folkenflik says that in the twenty-first century, CNN remains relevant. They continue to push other media outlets to do more with more stories in more places around the world. If the cable news networks relentlessly cover a story, other journalists are also encouraged to talk about it.

However, people's attention has shifted since the network and the twenty-four-hour news cycle started. "When crisis hits, people turn to cable, they particularly turn to CNN. And when crisis abates, they kind of tune it out. They don't need it as much." This has caused steep drops in ratings. So, according to Folkenflik, since the late 1990s, CNN "has engaged in kind of this leadership by revolving door where every 14 to 24 months you see somebody at the top kicked out and a brand-new grand philosophy announced. It's been an awkward time for them."

Tom Johnson, CNN's president during its rise to power in the early 1990s, has wondered if the concern lies deeper than the network's leadership. He has questioned the efficacy of the entire twenty-four-hour news cycle. "At what point should we show more restraint?" Johnson wonders. Nonstop news is "satisfying what is clearly a desire on the part of the viewers," he says, but "is that good journalism or is that just pandering?" He thinks that question is a "big issue for every journalist today." A major part of his career was made in television, but he still thinks there is "a wonderful place for print to look at things to be put into more context."

For Tom Shales, the *Washington Post* television critic when the *Challenger* space shuttle broke apart midflight, television is disruptive—but in an ultimately good way. "Very quickly," he wrote in 1986, "television reorders American life and creates American lore."

Chronology

1931 Rupert Murdoch, the founder of Fox News, is born in Melbourne, Australia.

1938 Ted Turner, the founder of CNN, is born in Cincinnati, Ohio.

1940 Cable technology becomes available.

1941 Tom Johnson, who led CNN through the first Gulf War, is born in Macon, Georgia.

1962 Walter Cronkite becomes the anchor of CBS *Evening News*.

1963 President John F. Kennedy is assassinated. His death changes how news networks view technology.

1979 C-SPAN launches. It airs twenty-four-hour coverage of US government sessions.

1980 Cable News Network (CNN) begins. Bernard Shaw becomes its first chief anchor.

1981 Dan Rather replaces Walter Cronkite as anchor of CBS *Evening News*. This is the first major "anchor war."

1984 US Congress passes the Cable Act.

1986 The space shuttle *Challenger* tragedy becomes a major twenty-four-hour news story.

1991 Operation Desert Storm begins. It becomes an important twenty-four-hour news story.

1994 O. J. Simpson is arrested. His trial for murder begins early the following year. Some call it the "trial of the century," thanks in part to the associated news coverage.

1997 Fox News broadcasts in-depth coverage of the investigation of Bill Clinton's reelection campaign.

Glossary

anchor The person who presents the news on a news program.

antitrust Legislation preventing monopolies in order to encourage competition that benefits consumers.

broadcast (noun) Television that is available free over the air with the proper antenna.

cable Television delivered by cable, and at a cost.

call sign Unique identifier for a network, starting in the United States with K for stations west of the Mississippi River and W east of the river.

clickbait Online content whose main purpose is to attract attention.

flog To tell a story so much that it becomes uninteresting.

infotainment Media that offers information ("info-") and entertainment ("-tainment").

media conglomerate A company that owns several media companies.

meme Image, video, piece of text, etc., that is copied and spread via the internet.

network Referring to broadcast TV, as opposed to cable TV.

parent company A company that owns enough stock in another company to control its management and operation.

public access Noncommercial mass media broadcast through cable channels and created by anyone, including the general public.

ratings Estimated audience size.

satellite Television broadcasting using a satellite to relay signals to customers in a particular area with special equipment.

sensationalist News stories that are more exciting or shocking than they are accurate.

simulcast A transmission of the same program on radio and television or on multiple channels at the same time.

superstation A television station that broadcasts widely.

twenty-four-hour news cycle A format in which news is covered twenty-four hours a day, as it happens.

Further Information

Books

Cohen, Jeffrey E. *The Presidency in the Era of 24-Hour News.* Princeton, NJ: Princeton University Press, 2008.

Dagnes, Alison. *Politics on Demand: The Effects of 24-Hour News on American Politics.* Santa Barbara, CA: ABC-CLIO, 2010.

Schieffer, Bob. *Overload: Finding Truth in Today's Deluge of News.* London, UK: Rowan and Littlefield, 2017.

Wiener, Robert. *Live from Baghdad.* New York: Doubleday, 1991.

Websites

CNN
http://www.cnn.com

On July 18, 2011, CNN became the first network to stream its twenty-four-hour news on its website and app.

Fox News

http://www.foxnews.com

Read articles, stream Fox News, and listen to Fox News Radio through the new giant's website.

PolitiFact

http://www.politifact.com

This Pulitzer Prize–winning website investigates claims made by politicians, reporters, and internet news sources.

Videos

"Breaking the News Cycle"

https://www.youtube.com/watch?v=aPZrxvSn8VM

Former news anchor Diana Fairbanks presents a critical look at how ratings influence the way news is reported.

"1986 Space Shuttle *Challenger* Explosion"

http://www.cnn.com/videos/us/2013/06/03/vault-backstory-1986-challenger-disaster.cnn/video/playlists/atv-moments-in-history

This short video shows the CNN newsroom immediately after the space shuttle explosion.

Bibliography

Appelbaum, Binyamin. "Joe Weisenthal vs. the 24-Hour News Cycle." *New York Times*, May 10, 2012. http://www.nytimes.com/2012/05/13/magazine/joe-weisenthal-vs-the-24-hour-news-cycle.html.

Barnard, Katherine Hollar. "Modern Media Tips: Working with Reporters in the 24-Hour News Cycle." *Forbes*, July 31, 2017. https://www.forbes.com/sites/forbesagencycouncil/2017/07/31/modern-media-tips-working-with-reporters-in-the-24-hour-news-cycle/#7eb2cbb11e8d.

Braestrup, Peter. "'Live from Baghdad': 'We're Using Them, They're Using Us.'" *New York Times*, January 5, 1992. http://www.nytimes.com/1992/01/05/books/wiener-live.html.

Bucy, Erik P., Walter Gantz, and Zheng Wang. "Media Technology and the 24-Hour News Cycle." In *Communication Technology and Social Change*, edited by Carolyn A. Lin and David J. Atkin, 143–157. Mahwah, NJ: Lawrence Erlbaum Associates, 2007.

Cate, Fred H. "'CNN Effect' Is Not Clear-Cut." *Humanitarian Affairs Review*, Summer 2002. https://www.globalpolicy.org/component/content/article/176/31233.html.

CNN. "Ted Turner Fast Facts." Last updated November 4, 2017. http://www.cnn.com/2013/06/10/us/ted-turner-fast-facts/index.html.

Cohen, Jeffrey E. *The Presidency in the Era of 24-Hour News.* Princeton, NJ: Princeton University Press, 2008.

de Moraes, Lisa. "Cronkite Says Schieffer Was Better Choice as CBS Anchor." *Washington Post*, March 8, 2005. http://www.washingtonpost.com/wp-dyn/articles/A15601-2005Mar7.html.

Diamond, Edwin. "Anchor Wars: Dan Rather, Peter Jennings and Tom Brokaw." *Rolling Stone*, October 9, 1986. https://www.rollingstone.com/tv/features/anchor-wars-19861009.

Escobedo, Tricia. "When a National Disaster Unfolded Live in 1986." CNN. Retrieved December 1, 2017. http://www.cnn.com/2016/03/31/us/80s-cnn-challenger-coverage/index.html.

Fishman, Margie. "Alum Maury Povich Talks on 'Infotainment.'" *Daily Pennsylvanian*, October 31, 1997. http://www.thedp.com/article/1997/10/alum_maury_povich_talks_on_infotainment.

Frank, Allan Dodds. "News Feud Escalates." CNN, October 11, 1996. http://money.cnn.com/1996/10/11/companies/tw_murdoch_pkg.

Galant, Richard. "The Most Trusted Man in America." CNN, June 5, 2012. http://www.cnn.com/2012/06/05/opinion/ brinkley-walter-cronkite/index.html.

Halbrooks, Glenn. "How TV News Has Evolved in the Past 50 Years." *Balance*, June 26, 2017. https://www. thebalance.com/a-look-at-tv-news-history-over-the-past-50-years-2315217.

Hansen, Liane, and David Folkenflik. "The Power of the 24-Hour News Cycle." NPR's *Weekend Edition Sunday*, May 29, 2005. https://www.npr.org/templates/story/ story.php?storyId=4671485.

Hewlett, Steve. "Why Britain Has Reason to Be Grateful to Rupert Murdoch." *Guardian*, April 27, 2013. https:// www.theguardian.com/media/2013/apr/28/rupert-murdoch-britain-grateful.

Hilliard, Robert L., and Michael C. Keith. *The Broadcast Century and Beyond: A Biography of American Broadcasting*. 5th ed. New York: Focal Press, 2010.

Hochfelder, David. "The Telegraph and the Origins of the 24-Hour News Cycle." *JHU Press Blog*, December 7, 2016. https://www.press.jhu.edu/news/blog/telegraph-and-origins-24-hour-news-cycle.

ICT Staff. "Osage Nation Takes Ownership of Ted Turner's 43,000-Acre Ranch." *Indian Country Today*, August 25, 2016. https://indiancountrymedianetwork.com/news/

business/osage-nation-takes-ownership-of-ted-turners-
43000-acre-ranch.

Kirby, Joseph A. "Mayor Takes Star Role in NYC Cable TV
War Between Media Giants." *Chicago Tribune*, October
18, 1996. http://articles.chicagotribune.com/1996-10-
18/news/9610180307_1_fox-news-channel-channel-
locked-time-warner.

Kurtz, Howard. "Bernard Shaw, Under Siege." *Washington
Post*, January 22, 1991. https://www.washingtonpost.
com/archive/lifestyle/1991/01/22/bernard-shaw-under-
siege/339c65c3-ff26-41fa-9ffe-8b274aae2fb0/?utm_
term=.fc014ae59414.

Marcus, David. "For Public Sanity's Sake, It's Time to Slow
the News Cycle." *Federalist*, December 5, 2017. https://
thefederalist.com/2017/12/05/public-sanitys-sake-time-
slow-news-cycle.

Martin, Michel. "Former CNN Anchor Kept Cool, but Paid
the Price of Success." NPR's *Tell Me More*, July 30,
2014. https://www.npr.org/2014/07/30/336538635/
former-cnn-anchor-bernard-shaw-kept-cool-but-paid-
the-price-of-success.

McDougal, Dennis. "How CNN Won Battle for a Phone
Line." *Los Angeles Times*, January 25, 1991. http://
articles.latimes.com/1991-01-25/entertainment/ca-
710_1_all-news-network.

Newton, Jim, and Shawn Hubler. "Simpson Held After Wild Chase: He's Charged with Murder of Ex-Wife, Friend." *Los Angeles Times*, June 18, 1994. http://www.latimes.com/local/la-oj-anniv-arrest-story.html.

Nicyski, Ron. "3 Ways to Set Up a Media Room in a 24-Hour News Cycle." *Adweek*, March 3, 2016. http://www.adweek.com/digital/3-ways-to-set-up-a-media-room-in-a-24-hour-news-cycle.

Nigut, Bill. "Former CNN President Tom Johnson on a Lifetime in Journalism." Georgia Public Broadcasting's *Two Way Street*, January 14, 2017. http://gpbnews.org/post/former-cnn-president-tom-johnson-lifetime-journalism.

Peabody Awards. "24 Hour Blizzard Coverage." Retrieved December 1, 2017. http://www.peabodyawards.com/award-profile/24-hour-blizzard-coverage.

Rogers, Tony. "Is Sensationalism in the News Bad?" *ThoughtCo.*, October 26, 2017. https://www.thoughtco.com/is-sensationalism-in-the-news-media-bad-2074048.

Rutenberg, Jim. "Fox Portrays a War of Good and Evil, and Many Applaud." *New York Times*, December 3, 2001. http://www.nytimes.com/2001/12/03/business/fox-portrays-a-war-of-good-and-evil-and-many-applaud.html.

Sambrook, Richard, and Sean McGuire. "Have 24-Hour TV News Channels Had Their Day?" *Guardian*, February 3, 2014. https://www.theguardian.com/media/2014/feb/03/tv-24-hour-news-channels-bbc-rolling.

Shedden, David. "Early TV Anchors." Poynter Institute, April 4, 2006. https://www.poynter.org/news/early-tv-anchors.

Siemaszko, Corky. "Roger Ailes: How 'Cruelest Lesson' Fueled Rise of Fox News Chief." NBC News, May 19, 2017. https://www.nbcnews.com/news/us-news/roger-ailes-how-cruelest-lesson-fueled-rise-fox-news-chief-n761676.

Stanley, Ben. "How New Zealand's Peter Arnett, the World's Greatest War Correspondent, Found Peace at Last." *Spinoff*, March 22, 2016. https://thespinoff.co.nz/media/22-03-2016/how-new-zealands-peter-arnett-the-worlds-greatest-war-correspondent-found-peace-at-last.

Times Higher Education. "The Rise of 24-Hour News Television: Global Perspectives." November 4, 2010. https://www.timeshighereducation.com/books/the-rise-of-24-hour-news-television-global-perspectives/414095.article.

Tryon, Chuck. "The Power of Political Memes." *Week*, August 23, 2016. http://theweek.com/articles/644312/power-political-memes.

Zak, Dan. "Thirty Years Ago, a TV Critic Watched the Challenger Explosion. This Is What He Saw." *Washington Post*, January 28, 2016. https://www.washingtonpost.com/news/arts-and-entertainment/wp/2016/01/28/thirty-years-ago-a-tv-critic-watched-the-challenger-explosion-this-is-what-he-saw.

Zarrella, John. "Zarrella on 25 Years Ago: 'We Realized That Something Was Really Wrong." *This Just In*, January 28, 2011. http://news.blogs.cnn.com/2011/01/28/zarrella-on-25-years-ago-we-realized-that-something-was-really-wrong.

Index

Page numbers in **boldface** are illustrations.

About the Author

Kristin Thiel lives in Portland, Oregon, where she is a writer and editor of books, articles, and documents for publishers, individuals, and businesses. She has worked on many of the books in the So, You Want to Be A … series, which offers career guidance for kids and is published by Beyond Words, an imprint of Simon & Schuster. She was the lead writer on a report for her city about funding for high school dropout prevention. Thiel has judged YA book contests and managed before-school and afterschool literacy programs for AmeriCorps VISTA.